Chapter 1: Ancient Dictatorships

The concept of dictatorship has been present throughout history, and in ancient times, many civilizations were ruled by a single person with absolute power. Some of the most famous ancient dictatorships include the Roman Empire, ancient Greece, and the various kingdoms of Asia.

In Rome, the dictatorship was a constitutional office that was granted to a single individual in times of crisis. This person was given absolute power over the Roman state for a period of six months, after which their power was relinquished. However, many dictators in ancient Rome abused their power and sought to extend their terms of office, leading to instability and conflict within the state.

One of the most famous Roman dictators was Julius Caesar, who came to power in 44 BC after defeating his political opponents in a civil war. Caesar quickly consolidated his power and began to implement a number of reforms, including the Julian calendar and the expansion of Roman citizenship. However, his growing power and popularity made him a threat to the traditional Roman elites, and he was assassinated in 44 BC.

In ancient Greece, the concept of dictatorship was slightly different from that of Rome. Greek dictators were often appointed to rule a city-state in times of crisis, such as during war or political instability. These dictators were usually given absolute power for a limited period of time and were expected to relinquish their power once the crisis had passed.

One of the most famous Greek dictators was Peisistratos of Athens, who came to power in the 6th century BC. Peisistratos ruled Athens with an iron fist and was known for his public works projects, including the construction of the Acropolis. However, his reign was also marked by political repression and the suppression of dissent.

In Asia, many kingdoms and empires were ruled by absolute monarchs who had complete control over their subjects. These rulers were often considered divine or semi-divine, and their power was seen as being bestowed by the gods.

One of the most famous ancient Asian dictators was Genghis Khan, the founder and first emperor of the Mongol Empire. Genghis Khan ruled over a vast empire that stretched from China to Eastern Europe, and he was known for his brutal tactics and military conquests. Under his rule, the Mongol Empire became one of the largest and most powerful in history.

In conclusion, ancient dictatorships were present in many civilizations throughout history, and the lives of the rulers who held absolute power over their subjects are fascinating and often terrifying. By examining these ancient dictatorships, we can gain a better understanding of the forces that drive people to seek absolute power, as well as the consequences of their rule for their respective societies and the world.

Chapter 2: European Dictatorships

In the 20th century, Europe was home to some of the most notorious dictatorships in history, particularly the fascist regimes of Italy, Spain, and Germany. These dictatorships were characterized by authoritarian rule, the suppression of political opposition, and the glorification of national identity and militarism.

One of the most infamous European dictators was Benito Mussolini, the leader of the fascist regime in Italy. Mussolini rose to power in the 1920s and implemented a totalitarian regime that suppressed political opposition and sought to establish Italy as a major European power. Under Mussolini's rule, Italy was involved in several military conflicts, including the invasion of Ethiopia and the Axis powers during World War II. However, Mussolini's regime was eventually overthrown in 1943, and he was executed by Italian partisans in 1945.

Another major European dictatorship was that of Francisco Franco in Spain. Franco came to power in 1939 following the Spanish Civil War, and his regime was characterized by the suppression of political opposition and the promotion of traditional Spanish values. Franco remained in power until his death in 1975, and his regime is remembered for its human rights abuses and repression of minority groups, particularly the Basques and Catalans.

Perhaps the most infamous European dictatorship was that of Adolf Hitler in Germany. Hitler rose to power in 1933 as the leader of the Nazi Party, and his regime was characterized by totalitarianism, antisemitism, and aggression towards neighboring countries. Under Hitler's rule, Germany invaded Poland, sparking World War II, and was responsible for the genocide of six million Jews during the Holocaust. Hitler's regime was ultimately defeated in 1945, but the impact of his rule continues to be felt to this day.

In addition to these fascist regimes, Europe also saw the rise of communist dictatorships in the 20th century, particularly in the Soviet Union and Eastern Europe. These regimes were characterized by the suppression of political opposition, the implementation of a planned economy, and the promotion of Marxist ideology.

One of the most infamous communist dictators was Joseph Stalin, who ruled the Soviet Union from the 1920s until his death in 1953. Stalin's regime was responsible for the deaths of millions of people through famine, forced labor, and political repression. Despite his brutal tactics, Stalin is still remembered by some as a hero of the Soviet Union, and his legacy continues to be debated to this day.

In conclusion, the European dictatorships of the 20th century were characterized by authoritarian rule, the suppression of political opposition, and the glorification of national identity and militarism. The impact of these regimes on Europe and the world at large continues to be felt to this day, and their legacies continue to be debated and studied by historians and scholars.

Chapter 3: Communist Dictatorships

Communist dictatorships have been a significant feature of modern history, particularly in the 20th century. These regimes were characterized by a one-party political system, the suppression of political opposition, the implementation of a planned economy, and the promotion of Marxist ideology.

One of the most well-known communist dictatorships was the Soviet Union under the leadership of Joseph Stalin. Stalin's regime was responsible for the deaths of millions of people through famine, forced labor, and political repression. Stalin's policies led to the creation of a planned economy and the collectivization of agriculture, resulting in widespread hardship and famine. Despite the negative impact of his rule, Stalin's legacy is still celebrated by some in Russia, where he is often viewed as a symbol of strength and determination.

Another well-known communist dictatorship was that of Mao Zedong in China. Mao's regime was characterized by a cult of personality, political repression, and the implementation of a planned economy. Mao's Great Leap Forward, which aimed to rapidly industrialize China, resulted in widespread famine and the deaths of millions of people. Mao's Cultural Revolution, which aimed to root out perceived enemies of the regime, also led to widespread violence and political repression.

Other communist dictatorships include North Korea under the Kim dynasty and Cuba under Fidel Castro. North Korea is known for its strict censorship, human rights abuses, and the cult of personality surrounding its leaders. Cuba, under Castro's rule, implemented a planned economy and strict censorship, but also made strides in improving healthcare and education for its citizens.

Despite the negative impacts of many communist dictatorships, some argue that they also brought positive change, particularly in terms of social welfare programs and the promotion of gender and racial equality. However, the suppression of political opposition, censorship, and human rights abuses associated with communist dictatorships have often led to widespread suffering and hardship for citizens.

In conclusion, communist dictatorships have been a significant feature of modern history, with some of the most notorious regimes characterized by political repression, the implementation of a planned economy, and the promotion of Marxist ideology. While some argue that these regimes brought positive change, the negative impacts of their rule, including censorship, human rights abuses, and widespread hardship, cannot be ignored.

Chapter 4: African and Middle Eastern Dictatorships

Dictatorships have been a common feature in Africa and the Middle East, with many of these regimes characterized by authoritarian rule, the suppression of political opposition, and the promotion of national identity and militarism.

One of the most notorious African dictators was Idi Amin, who ruled Uganda from 1971 to 1979. Amin's regime was characterized by political repression, human rights abuses, and the persecution of ethnic and religious minorities. Amin's regime was also responsible for the deaths of thousands of people, and he is remembered as one of the most brutal dictators in African history.

In the Middle East, Saddam Hussein was one of the most well-known dictators, having ruled Iraq from 1979 to 2003. Hussein's regime was characterized by political repression, human rights abuses, and the promotion of national identity and militarism. Hussein is also remembered for his brutal tactics, including the use of chemical weapons on his own people and the suppression of political opposition.

Another well-known African dictator was Muammar Gaddafi, who ruled Libya from 1969 to 2011. Gaddafi's regime was characterized by political repression, human rights abuses, and the promotion of national identity and militarism. Gaddafi is also remembered for his role in supporting terrorist organizations and his involvement in various military conflicts, including the civil war in Chad and the conflict in Darfur.

In recent years, other African and Middle Eastern countries have also experienced dictatorships, including Egypt, Syria, and Zimbabwe. These regimes have been characterized by political repression, censorship, human rights abuses, and the suppression of political opposition.

Despite the negative impacts of these dictatorships, there have also been movements for democracy and freedom in these regions. The Arab Spring, which began in 2010, saw protests and uprisings in several Middle Eastern and North African countries, with many people calling for greater political freedom and democracy. Similarly, in many African countries, there have been movements for greater political freedom and the establishment of democratic governments.

In conclusion, African and Middle Eastern dictatorships have been characterized by political repression, human rights abuses, and the promotion of national identity and militarism. While these regimes have caused significant suffering for many citizens, there have also been movements for democracy and freedom, suggesting that these regions may be on a path towards greater political freedom and human rights.

Chapter 5: Modern Dictatorships

Modern dictatorships have evolved from those of the past, with new tactics and technologies used to maintain control and suppress dissent. These regimes are often characterized by the suppression of political opposition, the manipulation of the media, and the use of technology to monitor citizens.

One of the most well-known modern dictators is Vladimir Putin, who has been the de facto leader of Russia since 1999. Putin's regime has been characterized by political repression, the manipulation of the media, and the use of technology to monitor citizens. Putin has also been accused of human rights abuses and the suppression of political opposition, with several critics and opponents facing imprisonment or even death.

Another modern dictator is Recep Tayyip Erdogan, the president of Turkey since 2014. Erdogan's regime has been characterized by political repression, the suppression of political opposition, and the manipulation of the media. Erdogan has also been accused of human rights abuses, particularly in the aftermath of the 2016 coup attempt, which led to the imprisonment and torture of thousands of people.

China, under the leadership of Xi Jinping, is another modern dictatorship that has been the focus of international attention. Xi's regime has been characterized by the suppression of political opposition, censorship, and the use of technology to monitor citizens. The Chinese government has also been accused of human rights abuses, particularly against Uighur Muslims in the Xinjiang region.

Other modern dictatorships include those in Belarus, Venezuela, and the Philippines. These regimes are characterized by political repression, the suppression of political opposition, and the use of technology to monitor citizens.

Despite the negative impacts of modern dictatorships, there have also been movements for democracy and freedom. The 2019 protests in Hong Kong, for example, were a response to the increasing authoritarianism of the Chinese government, and saw millions of people take to the streets to call for greater political freedom and democracy. Similarly, in Belarus, there have been widespread protests in response to the disputed 2020 presidential election and the subsequent crackdown on political opposition.

In conclusion, modern dictatorships have evolved from those of the past, with new tactics and technologies used to maintain control and suppress dissent. While these regimes are characterized by political repression, the manipulation of the media, and the use of technology to monitor citizens, there have also been movements for democracy and freedom, suggesting that there is still hope for a world where citizens can live freely and without fear of persecution.

Conclusion: Dictator Leaders of the World

Throughout history, dictator leaders have been a common feature in many parts of the world, from ancient times to the present day. These regimes have been characterized by political repression, the suppression of political opposition, and the promotion of national identity and militarism. While some dictatorships have been more brutal than others, they all share a common thread: a concentration of power in the hands of a single individual or group, at the expense of the rights and freedoms of ordinary citizens.

Despite the negative impacts of dictatorships, there have also been movements for democracy and freedom in many parts of the world. From the Arab Spring to the protests in Hong Kong and Belarus, citizens have shown that they are willing to stand up for their rights and challenge the status quo, even in the face of violent repression.

The world has made progress towards greater political freedom and democracy, but there is still much work to be done. As long as dictator leaders exist, citizens will continue to suffer from political repression, censorship, and human rights abuses. It is up to all of us to stand up for the rights and freedoms of all people, and to work towards a future where democracy and freedom are the norm, rather than the exception.

Dictator Leaders of the World

There have been many dictator leaders throughout history, some of the most notable ones include:

1. Adolf Hitler – Nazi leader of Germany from 1933 to 1945.
2. Joseph Stalin – Soviet leader from 1924 to 1953.
3. Mao Zedong – Chinese communist leader from 1949 to 1976.
4. Saddam Hussein – Iraqi leader from 1979 to 2003.
5. Kim Jong-il – North Korean leader from 1994 to 2011.
6. Muammar Gaddafi – Libyan leader from 1969 to 2011.
7. Idi Amin – Ugandan leader from 1971 to 1979.
8. Pol Pot – Cambodian leader from 1975 to 1979.
9. Augusto Pinochet – Chilean leader from 1973 to 1990.
10. Bashar al-Assad – Syrian leader since 2000.

It's worth noting that while these individuals are often referred to as "dictators," not all of them necessarily fit the same mold. Some, like Mao Zedong and Fidel Castro, were communist leaders who rose to power through revolutionary movements. Others, like Saddam Hussein and Muammar Gaddafi, were strongmen who came to power through military coups. Regardless of their specific backgrounds and methods of seizing and maintaining power, all of these leaders were characterized by their authoritarian and often oppressive rule over their respective countries.

Conclusion: Dictatorship has been a recurring theme throughout human history, and the lives of the leaders who have ruled over nations with an iron fist are fascinating and often horrifying. By examining the lives of these individuals, we can gain a better understanding of the forces that drive people to seek absolute power, as well as the consequences of their rule for their respective countries and the world.

Adolf Hitler – Nazi leader of Germany from 1933 to 1945

Adolf Hitler was a German politician and leader of the Nazi Party, who rose to power as Chancellor of Germany in 1933 and later became Führer in 1934. He led Nazi Germany during World War II and was responsible for numerous atrocities, including the Holocaust, in which millions of people, primarily Jews, were murdered.

Hitler was born in Austria in 1889 and moved to Germany as a young man. He became involved in politics after World War I and was a key figure in the rise of the Nazi Party in the 1920s. Hitler was appointed Chancellor of Germany in 1933 and quickly consolidated his power, passing laws that limited freedom of speech and the press, and repressing political opposition.

In 1939, Hitler ordered the invasion of Poland, which sparked World War II. Over the next few years, Nazi Germany conquered much of Europe, including France and the Soviet Union. During this time, Hitler oversaw the systematic persecution and extermination of millions of people, primarily Jews, in what came to be known as the Holocaust.

Hitler's leadership was characterized by his extreme nationalism, anti-Semitism, and militarism. He believed in the superiority of the Aryan race and sought to create a German empire that would dominate Europe. Hitler also believed that the Jews were a subhuman race that posed a threat to the purity of the Aryan race, and he implemented policies aimed at their extermination.

Hitler's regime came to an end in 1945, when Allied forces defeated Nazi Germany. Hitler committed suicide in his bunker in Berlin on April 30, 1945, as Allied troops closed in on the city. The legacy of Hitler and the Nazi Party is one of hatred, violence, and genocide. The atrocities committed under their leadership remain a dark stain on the history of Germany and the world, and serve as a reminder of the dangers of totalitarianism, nationalism, and hate.

Joseph Stalin – Soviet leader from 1924 to 1953

Joseph Stalin was a Soviet politician and dictator who served as the General Secretary of the Communist Party of the Soviet Union from 1922 until his death in 1953. He rose to power after the death of Vladimir Lenin and implemented policies that transformed the Soviet Union into a superpower.

Stalin's leadership was characterized by his authoritarianism and brutal tactics. He implemented policies of forced collectivization and industrialization, which led to widespread famine and the deaths of millions of people. Stalin also purged the Communist Party and the military of anyone who he considered a threat to his rule, resulting in the execution or imprisonment of millions of people.

During World War II, Stalin played a key role in the defeat of Nazi Germany. However, his leadership during the war was also marked by his willingness to sacrifice countless Soviet lives to achieve victory. Stalin's leadership style was also characterized by his paranoia and mistrust of others, which led to the execution of many of his own comrades.

After the war, Stalin's policies led to a deterioration of the Soviet economy and a decline in the standard of living for the Soviet people. His leadership style and policies also led to tensions with the West, which ultimately led to the Cold War.

Stalin's legacy is one of authoritarianism, brutality, and the suppression of individual freedoms. The policies he implemented had a profound impact on the Soviet Union and the world, and his leadership continues to be controversial and divisive. Despite his role in defeating Nazi Germany, his leadership remains a reminder of the dangers of totalitarianism and the importance of individual rights and freedoms.

Mao Zedong – Chinese communist leader from 1949 to 1976

Mao Zedong was a Chinese communist revolutionary who led the Communist Party of China (CPC) to victory against the Nationalists in 1949. He then became the Chairman of the Communist Party and the leader of the People's Republic of China until his death in 1976.

Mao's leadership was characterized by his promotion of socialist ideology and his attempts to transform Chinese society through radical policies. He implemented a series of Five-Year Plans aimed at modernizing the economy and transforming China into an industrial power. He also launched the Great Leap Forward in 1958, which aimed to rapidly industrialize China through the formation of agricultural communes and the use of backyard furnaces, but it resulted in a massive famine and millions of deaths.

Mao was also known for his political purges, particularly during the Cultural Revolution of 1966-1976, which sought to eliminate his perceived opponents and create a more egalitarian society. This period of upheaval was marked by widespread violence and the persecution of intellectuals, party officials, and those deemed "bourgeois."

Mao's leadership was also characterized by his anti-imperialist and anti-colonialist stance, which influenced his foreign policy. He sought to spread communist ideology and supported revolutionary movements around the world, particularly in Asia, Africa, and Latin America.

Despite his controversial legacy, Mao remains a revered figure in China, particularly among those who view him as a symbol of resistance against foreign domination and as a leader who helped to restore China's dignity and pride. However, his policies also had profound negative impacts on

China, particularly during the Cultural Revolution, which remains a dark period in China's history.

Saddam Hussein – Iraqi leader from 1979 to 2003

Saddam Hussein was the fifth President of Iraq, serving from 1979 until 2003. He rose to power through the Ba'ath Party, which he used to suppress political opposition and establish his authoritarian rule.

Saddam's leadership was characterized by his aggressive foreign policy and his attempts to assert Iraq's dominance in the region. He was involved in a long-standing conflict with Iran in the 1980s, which lasted for eight years and resulted in the deaths of hundreds of thousands of people. He also invaded Kuwait in 1990, which led to the Gulf War in 1991 and resulted in the imposition of UN sanctions on Iraq.

Saddam's regime was marked by his brutal tactics to suppress political opposition, including the use of torture and executions. He also promoted a personality cult around himself, with his image appearing on everything from currency to public buildings.

The US-led invasion of Iraq in 2003 led to Saddam's overthrow and capture. He was subsequently put on trial by an Iraqi tribunal and was executed in 2006 for crimes against humanity.

Saddam's leadership is widely regarded as one of the most oppressive in the modern Middle East. His regime was characterized by the suppression of individual rights and freedoms, the persecution of minority groups, and the use of extreme violence to maintain his grip on power. Despite his aggressive foreign policy, his invasion of Kuwait ultimately led to his downfall and the end of his regime.

Kim Jong-il – North Korean leader from 1994 to 2011

Kim Jong-il was the second leader of North Korea, serving as the country's Supreme Leader from 1994 until his death in 2011. He succeeded his father, Kim Il-sung, who had been the country's leader since its founding in 1948.

Kim's leadership was characterized by his authoritarian rule and his efforts to consolidate his power. He continued his father's "Juche" ideology, which emphasizes self-reliance and isolationism, and pursued a policy of military-first, which prioritized the military over other sectors of society.

During his time in power, Kim oversaw the development of North Korea's nuclear weapons program, which led to international condemnation and sanctions. He also presided over a period of famine in the 1990s, which is estimated to have caused the deaths of hundreds of thousands of people.

Kim's leadership was also marked by a cult of personality, which elevated him to the status of a demigod. His image and ideology were used to maintain control over the population and suppress any dissent.

After his death in 2011, Kim was succeeded by his son, Kim Jong-un, who has continued many of his policies. The regime in North Korea remains one of the most repressive in the world, with limited freedoms and widespread human rights abuses.

Muammar Gaddafi – Libyan leader from 1969 to 2011

Muammar Gaddafi was the leader of Libya from 1969 until his overthrow and death in 2011. He came to power through a military coup, overthrowing King Idris in 1969, and established a socialist state in Libya.

Gaddafi's leadership was characterized by his authoritarian rule and his efforts to create a unique form of socialism in Libya, which he called the "Third International Theory." He emphasized the role of direct democracy and people's committees, which were intended to give power to the people. However, these committees were often controlled by the regime and used to suppress dissent.

Gaddafi's foreign policy was often marked by his anti-Western stance, including his support for various militant groups and his attempts to acquire weapons of mass destruction. In 1988, Libya was accused of being behind the bombing of Pan Am Flight 103 over Lockerbie, Scotland, which killed 270 people. The country was subjected to UN sanctions as a result.

During the Arab Spring in 2011, Gaddafi faced widespread protests and uprisings. The regime responded with violence, and a civil war broke out in Libya. In August 2011, rebels seized control of the capital, Tripoli, and Gaddafi went into hiding. He was eventually captured and killed by rebel forces in October 2011.

Gaddafi's leadership is widely regarded as one of the most oppressive and repressive in the Middle East. His regime was characterized by the use of torture and extrajudicial killings to suppress dissent, as well as the absence of basic freedoms and human rights. Despite his efforts to create a unique form of socialism, his regime was marked by corruption, nepotism, and the concentration of power in the hands of a few.

Idi Amin – Ugandan leader from 1971 to 1979

Idi Amin was the president of Uganda from 1971 to 1979. He came to power through a military coup, overthrowing the government of Milton Obote, and established a brutal dictatorship in Uganda.

Amin's leadership was characterized by his authoritarian rule and his use of violence and terror to maintain control. He was notorious for his human rights abuses, including the killing and torture of political opponents, ethnic minorities, and anyone he deemed a threat to his regime.

Amin's foreign policy was marked by his attempts to establish himself as a pan-African leader and his support for various liberation movements in Africa. He expelled thousands of Ugandan Asians in 1972, seizing their property and assets, which led to international condemnation and sanctions.

Amin's regime was also characterized by corruption and economic mismanagement, which contributed to the decline of the Ugandan economy. His leadership led to the deaths of an estimated 300,000 Ugandans.

In 1979, Amin's regime was overthrown by a coalition of Tanzanian and Ugandan forces, and he fled into exile in Saudi Arabia. He remained in exile until his death in 2003.

Amin's leadership is widely regarded as one of the most brutal and oppressive in African history. His regime was characterized by the use of violence and terror to suppress dissent and maintain power, as well as the absence of basic freedoms and human rights. The legacy of his regime is still felt in Uganda today.

Pol Pot – Cambodian leader from 1975 to 1979

Pol Pot was the leader of Cambodia from 1975 to 1979, during which time he led the Khmer Rouge regime, a radical communist government that was responsible for one of the worst genocides in modern history.

Pol Pot's leadership was characterized by his extreme ideology and his efforts to create a utopian agrarian society in Cambodia. He sought to eliminate all traces of Western influence and create a society based on the principles of Maoism and the peasant-based communism of China.

In order to achieve this, Pol Pot's regime systematically targeted intellectuals, professionals, and anyone who was perceived as a threat to the regime, resulting in the deaths of an estimated 1.7 million people, or about a quarter of Cambodia's population at the time. This included those who were educated, religious leaders, and anyone with ties to the previous government.

Pol Pot's regime also forced the entire population to work on communal farms, with no access to education or healthcare, resulting in widespread starvation, disease, and suffering.

In 1979, Pol Pot's regime was overthrown by Vietnamese forces, and he fled into the jungle, where he continued to lead a guerrilla insurgency against the Vietnamese-backed government. He was eventually ousted from power by his own forces in 1997 and placed under house arrest. He died in 1998.

Pol Pot's leadership is widely regarded as one of the most brutal and oppressive in modern history. His regime was characterized by the use of violence, terror, and genocide to suppress dissent and maintain power, as well as the absence of basic freedoms and human rights. The legacy of his regime is still felt in Cambodia today.

Augusto Pinochet – Chilean leader from 1973 to 1990

Augusto Pinochet was the leader of Chile from 1973 to 1990. He came to power in a military coup that overthrew the democratically elected government of President Salvador Allende.

Pinochet's leadership was characterized by his authoritarian rule and his use of violence and terror to maintain control. He established a military government that was responsible for the killing, torture, and disappearance of thousands of Chileans who were deemed political opponents or threats to the regime.

During his time in power, Pinochet's regime implemented a series of neoliberal economic policies, which led to the privatization of state-owned industries, cuts to social programs, and the enrichment of a small elite at the expense of the rest of the population.

Pinochet's regime was also marked by corruption and the plundering of state resources, including the looting of public funds and the theft of land and property.

In 1988, under international pressure, Pinochet allowed a referendum on his rule, which resulted in a majority of Chileans voting for an end to his regime. He was replaced by a democratically elected government in 1990.

Pinochet's leadership is widely regarded as one of the most oppressive in Latin American history. His regime was characterized by the use of violence and terror to suppress dissent and maintain power, as well as the absence of basic freedoms and human rights. The legacy of his regime is still felt in Chile today.

Bashar al-Assad – Syrian leader since 2000

Bashar al-Assad has been the President of Syria since 2000, following the death of his father, Hafez al-Assad, who had been in power since 1971.

Assad's leadership has been characterized by his authoritarian rule and the use of violence and repression to maintain control over Syria. He has been widely criticized for his regime's brutal crackdown on dissent, which has resulted in the deaths of tens of thousands of Syrians and the displacement of millions.

The Syrian Civil War, which began in 2011 as a peaceful protest movement against Assad's government, has been one of the deadliest conflicts of the 21st century, with estimates of up to 500,000 people killed and millions displaced. Assad's regime has been accused of using chemical weapons, indiscriminate bombings, and torture against its own citizens, and has been condemned by the international community for its human rights abuses.

Assad's government has been supported by Russia and Iran, and has been opposed by the United States, European Union, and many Arab countries. The conflict has also drawn in numerous other regional and international actors, including Turkey, Israel, and various extremist groups.

Assad has remained in power despite years of civil war and international pressure, and his regime has made some gains in recent years, but the conflict continues to rage on and a political resolution remains elusive. The future of Syria and its people remains uncertain.

Conclusion: Dictatorship has been a recurring theme throughout human history, and the lives of the leaders who have ruled over nations with an iron fist are fascinating and often horrifying. By examining the lives of these individuals, we can gain a better understanding of the forces that drive people to seek absolute power, as well as the consequences of their rule for their respective countries and the world.

What is Shark Skin Suit?

A shark skin suit is a type of suit made from a fabric that mimics the texture of a shark's skin. The fabric used in these suits is often made from a blend of wool, mohair, and silk, which gives it a unique texture and sheen.

Historically, sharkskin suits were popular in the 1920s and 1930s, particularly in the United States, where they were seen as a symbol of status and sophistication. The suits were often worn by gangsters and other members of the criminal underworld, who valued their luxurious look and feel.

Today, sharkskin suits are less commonly worn, but they are still considered a stylish and sophisticated option for formal occasions. The texture of the fabric gives the suits a subtle shine that can help them stand out from other types of suits. However, it's worth noting that the use of actual shark skin in clothing is generally frowned upon due to ethical and environmental concerns, so modern sharkskin suits are made from synthetic materials.

"Thank You"

Shark Skin Suit: Dictator Leaders of the World